A Simple Rosary Book

Revised by Donal Foley

All booklets are published thanks to the generous support of the members of the Catholic Truth Society

CATHOLIC TRUTH SOCIETY

PUBLISHERS TO THE HOLY SEE

Contents

The Rosary in History...............................3

Rediscovering the Rosary..........................7

Explaining the Rosary.............................15
   I. The Joyful Mysteries............................ 21
   II. The Mysteries of Light 21
   III. The Sorrowful Mysteries....................... 21
   IV. The Glorious Mysteries 22

How to say the Rosary 23

The Five Joyful Mysteries.........................39

The Five Mysteries of Light 44

The Five Sorrowful Mysteries 51

The Five Glorious Mysteries 56

All rights reserved. First published 2014 by The Incorporated Catholic Truth Society, 40-46 Harleyford Road London SE11 5AY Tel: 020 7640 0042 Fax: 020 7640 0046. © 2014 The Incorporated Catholic Truth Society.

ISBN 978 1 86082 925 3

~ The Rosary in History ~

The power of the Rosary comes from the fact that it is a meditation on the Scriptures with Mary, since the Our Father is Jesus's own prayer given to his disciples when they had asked him how they should pray (*Mt* 6:9-13), and the first part of the Hail Mary is also Scriptural, being a compilation of part of the dialogue between Mary and the angel Gabriel at the Annunciation (*Lk* 1:28), combined with the exclamation made by Elizabeth during the Visitation (*Lk* 1:42).

The word Rosary means a crown of roses, that is, it is a spiritual bouquet given to the Blessed Virgin by those who pray to her.

Dominicans

According to tradition, St Dominic, the founder of the Order of Preachers or Dominicans, (1170-1221), preached a form of the Rosary in France at the time that the Albigensian heresy was devastating the Faith there. Tradition also has it that the Blessed Virgin herself appeared to him and asked for the practice of praying the Rosary as an antidote for heresy and sin, and certainly this traditional view has been accepted by a number of Popes over the centuries.

As time went on, the Dominican Alain de Roche began to establish Rosary Confraternities to promote the praying of the Rosary. The form of the Rosary we have today is believed to date from his time, that is, the fifteenth century. In succeeding centuries, saints and Popes have highly recommended the Rosary as being the greatest prayer in the Church after the Mass and Liturgy of the Hours.

The Mysteries of the Rosary were divided into three groups of fifties dedicated to the Joyful, Sorrowful and Glorious mysteries, and these fifteen mysteries were officially established by Pope Pius V in 1569.

There have been a number of important historical incidents in which the praying of the Rosary has played a vital part in bringing about success, and in particular the Battle of Lepanto. Pope Pius V called for Catholics to pray the Rosary for victory, and the Holy League fleet decisively defeated Ottoman naval forces at Lepanto in the eastern Mediterranean, thus preventing the invasion of Europe. Before the battle, the Rosary was recited by the Christian sailors, and after five hours of fighting they triumphed. Out of this victory came the Feast of the Holy Rosary, which is celebrated each year on 7 October.

The various Marian apparitions which took place during the nineteenth century, and particularly in France, did a great deal to revive Catholicism in Europe, with the apparitions at Lourdes - where Our Lady appeared holding a rosary on her arm - being the most prominent in this process.

The Popes

The power of the Rosary has been recognised by many recent Popes, and particularly by Pope Leo XIII (1878-1903), who did much to promote it. He was greatly aware of the dangerous way in which nineteenth century society was developing, and he saw that the best way to counteract this was to get the Catholic faithful to pray the Rosary. To this end he issued a record eleven encyclicals on it.

And more recently, in 1955, the power of the Rosary was dramatically shown when the Soviet Army voluntarily left Eastern Austria, which they had occupied after the Second World War. Fr Petrus Pavlicek, a Franciscan, organised a Rosary Crusade from 1946 onwards, which eventually had ten percent of the population of 7 million, that is, 700,000 Austrians, praying five decades of the Rosary daily for peace in the country. He also organised candlelit processions in Vienna with a pilgrim Virgin statue of Our Lady from Fatima. The result was that on 13th May 1955, it was announced that the Soviets were willing to withdraw from Austria and sign a peace treaty.

Pope Pius XII (1939-1958) was insistent, too, about the power and importance of the Rosary, as was his successor, St Pope John XXIII, who was particularly devoted to the Rosary, and said all fifteen mysteries daily. Pope Paul VI, too, was aware of the power of the Rosary, and recommended it very strongly in his Apostolic Exhortation, *Marialis Cultus*.

St Pope John Paul II, with his great devotion to Our Lady, was also very keen to promote the Rosary, and issued his own Apostolic Letter on it, *Rosarium Virginis Mariae*, in 2002. He also proclaimed the year from October 2002 to October 2003 the "Year of the Rosary", and instituted the new "Mysteries of Light".

Pope Benedict XVI, too, and Pope Francis, have also shown strong support for the Rosary. So it retains its power, and for the last one hundred and fifty years, the Popes have been urging the faithful to pray the Rosary, echoing the appeal of Our Lady of Fatima at each of her six apparitions in 1917, that we should pray the Rosary daily to bring peace to the world. She also described herself as the "Lady of the Rosary" at Fatima, thus underlining its importance for the Church and the world.

Rediscovering the Rosary

Why pray the Rosary?

The Rosary,[1] though clearly Marian in character, is at heart a prayer with Christ at the centre. It contains all the depth of the Gospel message in its entirety. With the Rosary we sit at the school of Mary and are led to contemplate the beauty of the face of Christ and to experience the depths of his love. Through the Rosary the faithful receive abundant grace, as though from the very hands of the Mother of the Redeemer.

To recite the Rosary is nothing other than to contemplate with Mary the face of Christ. The Rosary, reclaimed in its full meaning, goes to the very heart of Christian life; it offers a familiar yet fruitful spiritual and educational opportunity for personal contemplation, the formation of the People of God, and the new evangelisation. A prayer so easy and yet so rich truly deserves to be rediscovered by the Christian community - may we confidently take up the Rosary again, rediscover it in the light of Scripture, in harmony with the Liturgy, and in the context of our daily lives.

Rosary undervalued

There is in our time a great risk that the Rosary is undervalued and no longer taught to the younger generation. Some erroneously think that the centrality of the Liturgy necessarily entails giving less importance to the Rosary. But this prayer does not conflict with the Liturgy, but rather sustains it, serving as an excellent introduction to and echo of the Liturgy, enabling people to participate fully and interiorly in it and to reap its fruits in their daily lives. Nor is such a devotion, so clearly directed to the Christological centre of the Christian faith, to be considered as unecumenical - properly revitalised it is an aid and no hindrance to ecumenism.

A school of prayer

The most important reason for strongly encouraging the practice of the Rosary is that it represents a most effective means of fostering among the faithful that commitment to the contemplation of the Christian mystery, a genuine 'training in holiness': what is needed in a Christian life distinguished above all in 'the art of prayer'. The West is now experiencing a renewed demand for meditation, and in effect the Rosary is simply a method of contemplation, it serves as a means to an end and cannot become an end in itself, though never undervalued all the same. The Rosary is one of the finest traditions to have grown out of Christian contemplative prayer in the Christian West, comparable to the famous 'prayer of the heart' or 'Jesus prayer' of the Christian East.

Prayer for peace and for the family

Reviving the Rosary is important because of the great contemporary need to implore God for peace, by looking on Christ "who broke down the dividing wall of hostility". Anyone who assimilates the mystery of Christ - and this is clearly the goal of the Rosary - learns the secret of peace and makes it his life's project, giving birth to fruits of charity. The Rosary also makes of us peacemakers.

Such a revival in Christian families will also be an effective aid to countering the devastating effects of the menacing forces of disintegration playing on the institution of the family - so indispensable to the future of society. The family that prays together stays together. This is so true of the Rosary, which keeps alive lines of communication within families, where Jesus is placed at the centre. Even Mary herself, in the apparitions at Lourdes and Fatima exhorts us to make recourse to this prayer.

It is also beautiful and fruitful to entrust to this prayer the growth and development of children. Given the great range and gravity of seductions to be resisted by children today, the spiritual aid of praying the Rosary for children and even more with children, should not be underestimated.

Learning from Mary

The aim of the Rosary is to contemplate the face of Christ and no one has ever been devoted to contemplating the face of Christ as faithfully as Mary. Through the Rosary, we remember Christ with Mary, and 'learn Christ' from Mary. She was with Christ throughout his life, she carried him in her womb, brought him into the world in the stable, watched him grow up, preach, perform miracles, suffer and die and finally conquer death in the resurrection. She is the greatest and most perfect guide for us to the life of Jesus.

Saving power of the mysteries

Mary lived with her eyes fixed on Jesus, treasuring his every word, kept them and pondered them in her heart. The memories of Jesus, impressed on her heart, were always with her, leading her to reflect on the various moments of her life at her Son's side. In a way those memories were to be the 'rosary', which she

REDISCOVERING THE ROSARY

recited uninterruptedly throughout her earthly life. Mary constantly sets before us the 'mysteries' of her Son, with the desire that the contemplation of those mysteries will release all their saving power. In the recitation of the Rosary, the Christian community enters into contact with the memories and the contemplative gaze of Mary. Precisely because it starts with Mary's own experience, the Rosary is an exquisitely contemplative prayer. Without this contemplative dimension it would lose its meaning.

Mary's contemplation is above all a remembering, in the sense of 'a making present' of the works brought about by God in the history of salvation - to 'remember' them in a spirit of faith and love is to be open to the grace which Christ won for us by the mysteries of his life, death and resurrection. The Rosary in its own way too is part of the varied panorama of 'ceaseless prayer' called for by the great apostle Paul. By immersing us in the mysteries of the Redeemer's life, the Rosary ensures that what he has done and what the Liturgy makes present is profoundly assimilated and shapes our existence.

Being conformed to Christ

Christ is the supreme teacher, the revealer and the one revealed. It is not just a question of learning what he taught but of 'learning him'. In this regard we could have no better teacher than Mary. Contemplating the scenes of the Rosary in union with Mary is a means of learning from her to 'read' Christ, to discover his secrets and to understand his message. As we contemplate each mystery of her Son's life, she invites us to do as she did at the Annunciation; to ask humbly the questions which open us to the light, in order to end with the obedience of faith: Behold I am the handmaid of the Lord; be it done to me according to your word.

In the spiritual journey of the Rosary, based on the constant contemplation - in Mary's company - of the face of Christ, this demanding ideal of being conformed to him is pursued through an association, which could be described in terms of friendship. We are enabled to enter naturally into Christ's life and as it were to share his deepest feelings. In this process of being conformed to Christ in the Rosary, we entrust ourselves in a special way to the maternal care of the Blessed Virgin - she who is the perfect icon of the motherhood of the Church.

If Jesus, the one Mediator, is the Way of our prayer, then Mary, his purest and most transparent reflection, shows us the Way. In the Gospel, at Cana, we see the power of Mary's intercession as she makes known to Jesus the needs of others: "They have no wine". The Rosary is both meditation and supplication. Insistent prayer to the Mother of God is based on confidence that her maternal intercession can obtain all things from the heart of her Son.

A catechetical tool

The Rosary is also a path of proclamation and increasing knowledge, in which the mystery of Christ is presented again and again at different levels of the Christian experience. Its form is that of a prayerful and contemplative presentation, capable of forming Christians according to the heart of Christ - in this way it can present a significant catechetical opportunity which pastors should use to advantage. Today we are facing new challenges. Why should we not once more have recourse to the Rosary, with the same faith as those who have gone before us? The Rosary retains all its power and continues to be a valuable pastoral tool for every good evangeliser.

Rhythm of the Rosary

Meditation on the mysteries of Christ is proposed in the Rosary by means of a method of repetition designed to assist their assimilation, above all of the Hail Mary. By its nature the recitation of the Rosary calls for a quiet rhythm and a lingering pace, helping the individual to meditate on the mysteries of the Lord's life as seen through the eyes of her who was closest to the Lord. This is especially so when the Rosary is seen as an outpouring of that love which tirelessly returns to the person loved. Not only does Christ have a divine heart, rich in mercy and forgiveness, but also a human heart, capable of stirrings of affection. Although the repeated Hail Mary is addressed to Mary, it is to Jesus that the act of love is ultimately directed, with her and through her - and nourished by a desire to be conformed ever more completely to Christ.

~ Explaining the Rosary ~

Praying and meditating

The Holy Rosary is both meditation and supplication. Certain simple prayers are said while the mind and heart dwell on particular incidents of the life and death of our Lord Jesus Christ and his mother, Mary.

The Mysteries of the Rosary

These incidents in the lives of Jesus and Mary are set out in twenty named 'mysteries'. These are presented in four groups of five 'mysteries' each, which recall many significant events from the Gospels and of our salvation story. (See list on pages 21-22.)

Thus there are five 'Joyful mysteries' marked by the joy radiating from the event of the Incarnation, recalling the infancy and hidden ministry of Jesus. There are five 'Mysteries of Light' (or 'Luminous mysteries'), recalling how Jesus in the years of his public life proclaiming the kingdom of God, truly emerges as 'the light of the world'. Then there are five 'Sorrowful mysteries', which focus on the individual moments of the Passion and death of our Lord, revealing the culmination of God's love. Finally, there are five 'Glorious mysteries', which invite us to pass beyond death in order to gaze upon Christ's glory in the new life of the resurrection, and to relive the joy of the apostles and of Mary. In so doing we rediscover the reasons for our own faith.

Praying with rosary beads

The Rosary is said with the help of rosary beads. This collection of fifty-nine small beads on a short, circular cord or chain, is divided into five groups of ten beads each. Each of these groups of ten beads (commonly known as a 'decade') is separated by an additional, dividing bead. Thus, the Rosary is said to consist of 'five decades'. Added to this circle, is a smaller, single group of five beads, at the end of which is usually attached a small crucifix.

These beads mark the different prayers said during the Rosary. The beads grouped into tens are the 'Hail Marys', when the Hail Mary prayer is repeated ten times during each 'decade'. The beginning and end of each decade is marked by the other single bead, which both indicates when the 'Our Father' is said at the start of a decade, and the 'Glory Be' at the close of a decade.

Rosary ring

Also popular is the use of a rosary 'ring', small enough to fit comfortably on the finger. The rosary ring carries only one 'decade' of ten small grooves or notches, with a small dividing marker, often in the form of a cross.

Praying the Mysteries of the Rosary

To pray the Rosary usually means to pray 'five decades' of the Rosary, and so involves saying the 'Our Father', followed by ten 'Hail Marys' and then the 'Glory Be' - this is repeated five times altogether.

While marking each prayer that is being said by passing the beads through the fingers, time is given to meditating on the particular theme attached to each of the 'decades' being prayed. These themes are described in 'the five mysteries' chosen, whether the Joyful, Luminous, Sorrowful or Glorious mysteries. If you choose the Joyful mysteries, for example, the first of the five mysteries, The Annunciation, is the theme to meditate on during the first decade. The second mystery, The Visitation, attaches to the second decade, and so on until the fifth mystery and decade (see page 22).

Aids to saying the Rosary

Announcing each 'mystery' is important, as the words direct the imagination and mind towards a particular episode in the life of Christ, opening up a scenario to focus our attention. It is often helpful to use icons and holy images to help to do this, and this corresponds to the inner logic of the Incarnation, that is, they are concrete aids to prayer. It is also most helpful to follow the announcement with the proclamation of a relevant scripture passage, providing a biblical foundation and greater depth to our meditation. So God is allowed to speak and we listen in silence (see page 39).

Customs attached to the Rosary

Whereas the usual practice is that people tend to say one set of mysteries on given days of the week, some people may wish to pray all of these four sets of mysteries together. In that case, after the Joyful mysteries the round of beads is said a further time, while the Luminous mysteries are contemplated, and thereafter the Sorrowful and Glorious mysteries too.

In current practice the 'Glory be' between each decade, is followed by a short concluding prayer, which varies according to local custom. The best form is one that prays for the fruits specific to that particular mystery. In this way the Rosary better expresses its connection with Christian life.

There is also a popular custom of expressing particular 'intentions' to be prayed for during the recitation of the Rosary, commonly prior to each new decade. These intentions may touch on a range of concerns affecting the Church and the world, or be of a more personal and immediate nature.

A variety of customs exist concerning the practical recitation of the Rosary. Where two or more pray the Rosary together, they may choose one to 'lead' each decade - that is, the one leading announces the mystery (and an 'intention' if appropriate) and says the first part of each prayer, to which the others respond with the second part. Alternatively, they may take it in turns to 'lead' and to respond; similar arrangements can be made for larger groups.

Mysteries said on certain days

Traditionally, different mysteries of the Rosary have been allocated to different days of the week. There are no strict rules, but a recommended practice is as follows:

The Joyful Mysteries:	*Mondays, Saturdays*
The Luminous Mysteries:	*Thursdays*
The Sorrowful Mysteries:	*Tuesdays, Fridays*
The Glorious Mysteries:	*Wednesdays, Sundays*

Customary changes to this pattern may arise during certain liturgical seasons of the year. So for example on the Sundays during Advent and Christmas the Joyful mysteries are often said, and in a similar way, the Sorrowful mysteries on Sundays during Lent, and the Glorious mysteries on the Sundays of Eastertide.

Beginning and ending the Rosary

At present, in different parts of the Church there are many ways to introduce the Rosary, some including the saying of the Creed as if to make the profession of faith the basis of the contemplative journey about to be undertaken.

The Rosary usually begins with prayers for the intentions of The Pope, as if to expand the vision of the one praying to embrace all the needs of the Church. To encourage this ecclesial dimension of the Rosary, the Church has seen fit to grant indulgences to those who recite it with the required dispositions (see further, page 39).

The small, single group of five beads (at the end of which is usually attached a small crucifix) normally indicates these additional prayers, which are usually said at the beginning of the Rosary.

The conclusion of the Rosary

Since the Rosary is truly a spiritual itinerary in which Mary acts as Mother, Teacher and Guide, it concludes with the opportunity for the grateful heart to burst forth in praise of the Blessed Virgin by praying either the 'Hail Holy Queen' (*Salve Regina*) or the Litany of Loreto. The choice of some of these prayers is guided by the liturgical season.

Explaining the Rosary

To pray the Rosary is nothing other than to contemplate with Mary the face of Christ.

I. The Joyful Mysteries

1. The Annunciation;
2. The Visitation;
3. The Nativity;
4. The Presentation in the Temple;
5. The Finding of the Child Jesus in the Temple.

II. The Mysteries of Light

1. The Baptism in the Jordan;
2. The Wedding at Cana;
3. The Proclamation of the Kingdom of God;
4. The Transfiguration;
5. The Institution of the Eucharist.

III. The Sorrowful Mysteries

1. The Agony in the Garden;
2. The Scourging at the Pillar;
3. The Crowning with Thorns;
4. The Carrying of the Cross;
5. The Crucifixion and Death of our Lord.

IV. The Glorious Mysteries

1. The Resurrection;

2. The Ascension of Christ into Heaven;

3. The Descent of the Holy Spirit;

4. The Assumption of Our Lady into Heaven;

5. The Coronation of Our Lady in Heaven and the Glory of the Saints.

~ How to say the Rosary ~

Begin the Rosary by holding and kissing the small crucifix attached to the end of the beads and making the sign of the cross, saying:

In the name of the Father, and of the Son, and of the Holy Spirit. Amen.
or
V. O God, come to our aid.
R. O Lord, make haste to help us.
Then say:

The Apostles' Creed

I believe in God,
the Father Almighty
Creator of heaven and earth.
and in Jesus Christ, his only Son, Our Lord, (*all bow*)
who was conceived by the Holy Spirit,
born of the Virgin Mary,
suffered under Pontius Pilate,
was crucified, died, and was buried;
he descended into hell;
on the third day he rose again from the dead;
he ascended into heaven,

and is seated at the right hand of God
the Father Almighty;
from there he will come again to judge the living
   and the dead.
I believe in the Holy Spirit,
the holy catholic Church,
the communion of saints,
the forgiveness of sins,
the resurrection of the body,
and life everlasting. Amen.

Then, for the intentions of the Pope, on the first bead after the crucifix say the 'Our Father'; on the following three beads say three 'Hail Marys, then say a 'Glory be' on the last bead remaining before the junction with the main circlet.

The name of the first mystery to be meditated is announced. Preferably, a related passage of Scripture (see page 39) is then proclaimed (length depending on the circumstances). As we listen we are certain that this is the Word of God, spoken for today and spoken 'for me' - we allow God to speak. In certain solemn communal celebrations this word can be appropriately illustrated by a brief commentary.

Pause - listening and meditation are nourished by silence.

How to say the Rosary

After listening to the word and focusing on the mystery, it is natural for the mind to be lifted upwards towards the Father. Jesus always leads us to the Father, so we say:

The Lord's Prayer

Our Father, who art in heaven,
hallowed be thy name.
Thy kingdom come.
Thy will be done on earth, as it is in heaven.

Give us this day our daily bread, and
forgive us our trespasses,
as we forgive those who trespass against us, and
lead us not into temptation,
but deliver us from evil. Amen.

Then say the Hail Mary (ten times), the centre of gravity of which is the name of Jesus.

The Hail Mary

Hail, Mary, full of grace, the Lord is with thee:
blessed art thou among women,
and blessed is the fruit of thy womb, Jesus.

Holy Mary, Mother of God, pray for
us sinners, now,
and at the hour of our death.
Amen.

Then say the Glory Be. The Trinitarian doxology (short hymn of praise) reminds us that unity with the Holy Trinity is the goal of all Christian contemplation. It is important that this high point is given due prominence in the Rosary. In public recitation it could be sung, to emphasise the crucial importance of Trinitarian praise.

The Glory Be

Glory be to the Father, and to the Son, and to the Holy Spirit:

as it was in the beginning, is now,
and ever shall be, world without end,
Amen.

Then a prayer at the conclusion of each decade for the fruits specific to that particular mystery may be said; for example:

O God, by meditating on this mystery, may we both imitate what it contains and obtain what it promises, through Christ Our Lord.

or

O my Jesus, forgive us our sins, save us from the fires of hell, lead all souls to heaven, especially those in most need of thy mercy.

This second prayer was given by Our Lady at Fatima, on 13th July 1917, and so it is particularly appropriate that it be said at the end of each mystery.

Now pass on to announcing and praying the second mystery in the same way as above. When all the mysteries have been said, then recite the following concluding prayers:

Hail Holy Queen - Salve Regina
(Normally said during Ordinary Time)

Hail, Holy Queen, Mother of mercy.
Hail, our life, our sweetness, and our hope.
To you do we cry, poor banished children of Eve;
to you do we send up our sighs,
mourning and weeping in this vale of tears. Turn, then, most gracious advocate,
your eyes of mercy toward us;
and after this our exile,
show unto us the blessed fruit of your womb, Jesus. O clement, O loving, O sweet Virgin Mary.

V. Pray for us, O Holy Mother of God
R. That we may be made worthy of the promises
of Christ.

V. Let us pray:

O God, whose only-begotten Son by his life, death and resurrection
has purchased for us the rewards of eternal life;
grant, we beseech you, that meditating on these
Mysteries of the most Holy Rosary of the Blessed Virgin Mary we may both imitate what they contain
and obtain what they promise, through the same Christ our Lord.

R. Amen.

Regina Caeli
(Normally said during Eastertide)

O Queen of heaven rejoice! Alleluia
For he whom you did merit to bear. Alleluia
Has risen as he said. Alleluia
Pray for us to God. Alleluia
V. Rejoice and be glad O Virgin Mary. Alleluia
R. For the Lord has risen indeed. Alleluia

Let us pray:

God our Father you gave joy to the world by the resurrection of your Son, Our Lord Jesus Christ. Through the prayers of his mother, the Virgin Mary, bring us to the happiness of eternal life. We ask this through Our Lord Jesus Christ your Son who lives and reigns with you and the Holy Spirit, one God for ever and ever. Amen.

Alma Redemptoris

(Normally said during Advent)

Loving Mother of the Redeemer, gate of heaven, star of the sea, assist your people who have fallen, as we strive to rise again.

To the wonderment of nature, you bore your Creator,
Yet remained a virgin as before.
You who received Gabriel's joyful greeting,
Have pity on us poor sinners.

Then the following Marian Litany may be said:

The Litany of the Loreto

Lord have mercy.
Lord have mercy.
Christ have mercy.
Christ have mercy.
Lord have mercy.
Lord have mercy.
Christ hear us.
Christ graciously hear us.

God the Father of heaven,
have mercy on us.
God the Son, Redeemer of the world,
have mercy on us.
God the Holy Spirit,
have mercy on us.
Holy Trinity, one God,
have mercy on us.

Holy Mary,
pray for us.
Holy Mother of God,
pray for us.
Holy Virgin of virgins,
pray for us.
Mother of Christ,
pray for us.
Mother of divine grace,
pray for us.
Mother most pure,
pray for us.
Mother most chaste,
pray for us.
Mother inviolate,
pray for us.
Mother undefiled,
pray for us.
Mother most lovable,
pray for us.
Mother most admirable,
pray for us.
Mother of good counsel,
pray for us.
Mother of our Creator,
pray for us.
Mother of our Saviour,
pray for us.
Virgin most prudent,
pray for us.
Virgin most venerable,
pray for us.
Virgin most renowned,
pray for us.
Virgin most powerful,
pray for us.
Virgin most merciful,
pray for us.
Virgin most faithful,
pray for us.
Mirror of justice,
pray for us.
Seat of wisdom,
pray for us.
Cause of our joy,
pray for us.
Spiritual vessel,
pray for us.
Vessel of honour,
pray for us.

How to say the Rosary

Singular vessel of devotion,
pray for us.
Mystical rose,
pray for us.
Tower of David,
pray for us.
Tower of ivory,
pray for us.
House of gold,
pray for us.
Ark of the covenant,
pray for us.
Gate of heaven,
pray for us.
Morning star,
pray for us.
Health of the sick,
pray for us.
Refuge of sinners,
pray for us.
Comfort of the afflicted,
pray for us.
Help of Christians,
pray for us.
Queen of Angels,
pray for us.
Queen of Patriarchs,
pray for us.
Queen of Prophets,
pray for us.
Queen of Apostles,
pray for us.
Queen of Martyrs,
pray for us.
Queen of Confessors,
pray for us.
Queen of Virgins,
pray for us.
Queen of all Saints,
pray for us.
Queen conceived
without original sin,
pray for us.
Queen assumed
into heaven,
pray for us.
Queen of the
most Holy Rosary,
pray for us.

Queen of the Family, *pray for us.*

Queen of Peace, *pray for us.*

Lamb of God, you take away the sins of the world,
spare us, O Lord.
Lamb of God, you take away the sins of the world,
graciously hear us, O Lord.
Lamb of God, you take away the sins of the world,
have mercy on us.
V. Pray for us, O holy Mother of God.
R. That we may be made worthy of the promises of Christ.

Let us pray:

Lord God, give to your people the joy of continual health in mind and body. With the prayers of the Virgin Mary to help us, guide us through the sorrows of this life to eternal happiness in the life to come. Grant this through our Lord Jesus Christ, your Son, who lives and reigns with you and the Holy Spirit, one God, for ever and ever.
R. Amen.

The Rosary finishes with the final sign of the cross.

Other Suitable Prayers

The Memorare

Remember, O most gracious Virgin Mary,
that never was it known that anyone
who fled to thy protection,
implored thy help, or sought thy intercession,
 was left unaided.
Inspired by this confidence I fly unto thee,
O Virgin of virgins, my Mother.
To thee do I come, before thee I stand,
 sinful and sorrowful.
O Mother of the Word Incarnate,
despise not my petitions,
but in thy mercy hear and answer me.
Amen.

We Fly to Thy Protection - *Sub Tuum Praesidium*

We fly to thy protection, O holy Mother of God, despise not our petitions in our necessities, but deliver us always from all dangers, O glorious and blessed Virgin.

Prayer for England

O Blessed Virgin Mary, Mother of God, and our most gentle queen and mother, look down in mercy upon England, your dowry, and upon us all who greatly hope and trust in you. By you it was that Jesus, our Saviour and our hope, was given to the world; and he has given you to us that we may hope still more.

Plead for us your children, whom you received and accepted at the foot of the cross, O Mother of sorrows. Pray for our separated brethren, that in the one true fold of Christ, we may all be united under the care of Pope N., the chief shepherd of Christ's flock. Pray for us all, dear mother, that by faith, and fruitful in good works, we may all deserve to see and praise God, together with you in our heavenly home.

Prayer to St Michael

St Michael, the Archangel, defend us in the day of battle; be our safeguard against the wickedness and snares of the devil. May God rebuke him, we humbly pray and do you, O Prince of the heavenly host, by the power of God, cast into hell Satan and all the other evil spirits who prowl through the world seeking the ruin of souls. Amen.

Prayer for the Pope

O almighty and eternal God, have mercy on your servant our Holy Father, the Pope, and direct him according to your clemency into the way of everlasting salvation; that he may desire by your grace those things that are agreeable to you, and perform them with all his strength. Through Christ our Lord. Amen.

Prayer for Priests

Father, you have appointed your Son Jesus Christ eternal High Priest. Guide those he has chosen to be ministers of word and sacrament and help them to be faithful in fulfilling the ministry they have received. Grant this through our Lord Jesus Christ, your Son, who lives and reigns with you and the Holy Spirit, one God, for ever and ever. Amen.

Prayer for Vocations

Lord Jesus Christ, shepherd of souls, who called the apostles to be fishers of men, raise up new apostles in your holy Church. Teach them that to serve you is to reign: to possess you is to possess all things. Kindle in the young hearts of our sons and daughters the fire of zeal for souls. Make them eager to spread your kingdom on earth. Grant them courage to follow you, who are the Way, the Truth and the Life; who live and reign for ever and ever. Amen.

Litany of Humility

O Jesus meek and humble of heart, *Hear me.*
From the desire of being esteemed,
Deliver, me, Jesus.

From the desire of being loved, *Deliver me, Jesus.*
From the desire of being extolled, *Deliver me, Jesus.*
From the desire of being honoured, *Deliver me, Jesus.*
From the desire of being praised, *Deliver me, Jesus.*
From the desire of being preferred to others,
   Deliver me Jesus.
From the desire of being consulted, *Deliver me, Jesus.*
From the desire of being approved, *Deliver me, Jesus.*
From the fear of being humiliated, *Deliver me, Jesus.*
From the fear of being despised, *Deliver me, Jesus.*
From the fear of suffering rebukes, *Deliver me, Jesus.*
From the fear of being calumniated, *Deliver, me, Jesus.*
From the fear of being forgotten, *Deliver me, Jesus.*
From the fear of being ridiculed, *Deliver me, Jesus.*
From the fear of being wronged, *Deliver me, Jesus.*
From the fear of being suspected, *Deliver me, Jesus.*

That others may be loved more than I,
Jesus, grant me the grace to desire it.
That others may be esteemed more than I,
Jesus, grant me the grace to desire it.

That, in the opinion of the world others may increase and I may decrease,
Jesus, grant me the grace to desire it.
That others may be chosen and I set aside,
Jesus, grant me the grace to desire it.
That others may be praised and I unnoticed,
Jesus, grant me the grace to desire it.
That others may be preferred to me in everything,
Jesus, grant me the grace to desire it.
That others may become holier than I, provided that I may become as holy as I should,
Jesus, grant me the grace to desire it.

(*Rafael Cardinal Merry del Val, 1865-1930*)

Indulgences

A plenary indulgence may be gained, under the usual conditions for the recitation of the Rosary (five decades are sufficient), in a church or public oratory or in the family. If the Rosary is said privately a partial indulgence may be gained. An indulgence is a remission granted by the Church to those who are free from the guilt of mortal sin, of the whole, or of a part, of the temporal punishment due for sins already forgiven. The usual conditions for gaining a plenary indulgence are, in addition to the good work to which it is attached:

(1) Confession on the day itself, or within some days before or after the performance of the good work. (2) Holy Communion on the day itself, or within some days before or after the performance of the good work. (3) Prayer for the intention of the Pope. For this, recitation of one Our Father and one Hail Mary suffices, though the faithful have the liberty of saying any other prayer according to their personal piety.

⁓ Scripture Passages ⁓
The Five Joyful Mysteries

The First Mystery: The Annunciation

In the sixth month the angel Gabriel was sent by God to a town in Galilee called Nazareth, to a virgin betrothed to a man named Joseph, of the house of David; and the virgin's name was Mary. He went in and said to her,

"Rejoice, so highly favoured! The Lord is with you." She was deeply disturbed by these words and asked herself what this greeting could mean, but the angel said to her, "Mary, do not be afraid; you have won God's favour. Listen! You are to conceive and bear a son, and you must name him Jesus. He will be great and will be called Son of the Most High. The Lord God will give him the throne of his ancestor David; he will rule over the house of Jacob for ever and his reign will have no end." Mary said to the angel, "But how can this come about, since I am a virgin?" "The Holy Spirit will come upon you" the angel answered, "and the power of the Most High will cover you with its shadow. And so the child will be holy and will be called Son of God. Know this too: your kinswoman Elizabeth has, in her old age, herself conceived a son, and she whom people called barren is now in her sixth month, for nothing is impossible to God." "I am the handmaid of the Lord," said Mary, "let what you have said be done to me." And the angel left her. (*Lk* 1:26-38)

The Second Mystery: The Visitation

Mary set out at that time and went as quickly as she could to a town in the hill country of Judah. She went into Zechariah's house and greeted Elizabeth. Now as soon as Elizabeth heard Mary's greeting, the child leapt in her womb and Elizabeth was filled with the Holy Spirit. She gave a loud cry and said, "Of all women you are the most blessed, and blessed is the fruit of your womb. Why should I be honoured with a visit from the mother of my Lord? For the moment your greeting reached my ears, the child in my womb leapt for joy. Yes, blessed is she who believed that the promise made her by the Lord would be fulfilled." (*Lk* 1:39-45)

The Third Mystery: The Nativity

Now at this time Caesar Augustus issued a decree for a census of the whole world to be taken. This census - the first - took place while Quirinius was governor of Syria, and everyone went to his own town to be registered. So Joseph set out from the town of Nazareth in Galilee and travelled up to Judaea, to the town of David called Bethlehem, since he was of David's House and line, in order to be registered together with Mary, his betrothed, who was with child. While they were there the time came for her to have her child, and she gave birth to a son, her first-born. She wrapped him in swaddling clothes, and laid him in a manger because there was no room for them at the inn. (*Lk* 2:1-7)

The Fourth Mystery: The Presentation in the Temple

And when the day came for them to be purified as laid down by the Law of Moses, they took him up to Jerusalem to present him to the Lord - observing what stands written in the Law of the Lord: Every first-born male must be consecrated to the Lord - and also to offer in sacrifice, in accordance with what is said in the Law of the Lord, a pair of turtledoves or two young pigeons. Now in Jerusalem there was a man named Simeon. He was an upright and devout man; he looked forward to Israel's comforting and the Holy Spirit rested on him. It had been revealed to him by the Holy Spirit that he would not see death until he had set eyes on the Christ of the Lord. Prompted by the Spirit he came to the Temple; and when the parents brought in the child Jesus to do for him what the Law required, he took him into his arms and blessed God; and he said: "Now, Master, you can let your servant go in peace, just as you promised; because my eyes have seen the salvation which you have prepared for all the nations to see, a light to enlighten the pagans and the glory of your people Israel". As the child's father and mother stood there wondering at the things that were being said about him, Simeon blessed them and said to Mary his mother, "You see this child: he is destined for the fall and for the rising of many in Israel, destined to be a sign that is rejected - and a sword will pierce your own soul too - so that the secret thoughts of many may be laid bare." (*Lk* 2:22-35)

The Fifth Mystery:
The Finding of the Child Jesus in the Temple

Every year his parents used to go to Jerusalem for the feast of the Passover. When he was twelve years old, they went up for the feast as usual. When they were on their way home after the feast, the boy Jesus stayed behind in Jerusalem without his parents knowing it. They assumed he was with the caravan, and it was only after a day's journey that they went to look for him among their relations and acquaintances. When they failed to find him they went back to Jerusalem looking for him everywhere. Three days later, they found him in the Temple, sitting among the doctors, listening to them, and asking them questions; and all those who heard him were astounded at his intelligence and his replies. They were overcome when they saw him, and his mother said to him, "My child, why have you done this to us? See how worried your father and I have been, looking for you." "Why were you looking for me?" he replied. "Did you not know that I must be busy with my Father's affairs?" But they did not understand what he meant. He then went down with them and came to Nazareth and lived under their authority. His mother stored up all these things in her heart. And Jesus increased in wisdom, in stature, and in favour with God and men. (*Lk* 2:41-52)

~ The Five Mysteries of Light ~

Introduction

The fifteen mysteries, - five Joyful, Sorrowful and Glorious, - were never meant to be exhaustive, and Jesus's public ministry between his baptism and his Passion had never featured at all in the traditional pattern of the prayer. During these years of public ministry, the mystery of Christ is most evidently a mystery of light: "While I am in the world, I am the light of the world". The five 'luminous' mysteries (or Mysteries of Light) introduced by Pope St John Paul II in 2002[2] bring out more fully the Christ-centred core of the prayer. Each of these is a revelation of the kingdom now present in the very person of Jesus:

1. His baptism in the River Jordan: he descends into waters, the innocent one who became 'sin' for our sake; the heavens open and the voice of the Father declares him the Beloved Son while the Spirit descends to invest him with his Mission (cf. *2 Co* 5:21; *Mt* 3:17).

2. His self-manifestation at the wedding in Cana: when he changes water into wine, he opens the hearts

The Five Mysteries of Light

of the disciples thanks to the intervention of Mary, the first among believers. "Do whatever he tells you" - this counsel is a fitting introduction to the words and signs of Christ's public ministry, and forms the Marian foundation of all the mysteries of light.

3. His proclamation of the kingdom of God, with his call to conversion: he does this by his preaching, and he forgives the sins of all who draw near to him in humble trust. It is the inauguration of the ministry of mercy which he continues to exercise until the end of the world, particularly through the Sacrament of Reconciliation which he has entrusted to his Church (cf. *Mk* 1:5; 2:3-13; *Lk* 7:47-48). One is put in mind of Pope St John XXIII convening the Second Vatican Council to renew the Church using "The medicine of mercy".

4. His Transfiguration when he revealed his glory to the apostles: The Transfiguration is the most luminous mystery of light. The glory of the Godhead shines forth from the face of Christ as the Father commands the astonished apostles to "listen to him", and prepare to experience with him the agony of the Passion so as to come with him to the joy of the resurrection, and a life transfigured by the Holy Spirit (cf. *Lk* 9:35-36).

5. His Institution of the Eucharist as the sacramental expression of the paschal mystery: Christ offers his Body and Blood as food under the sign of bread and wine, and testifies to the end, his love for humanity for whose salvation he will offer himself in sacrifice.[2]

The First Mystery: The Baptism of the Lord

Then Jesus appeared: he came from Galilee to the Jordan to be baptised by John. John tried to dissuade him. "It is I who need baptism from you," he said, "and yet you come to me!" But Jesus replied, "Leave it like this for the time being; it is fitting that we should, in this way, do all that righteousness demands." At this, John gave in to him. As soon as Jesus was baptised he came up from the water, and suddenly the heavens opened and he saw the Spirit of God descending like a dove and coming down on him. And a voice spoke from heaven, "This is my Son, the Beloved; my favour rests on him". (*Mt* 3:13-17)

The Second Mystery: The Wedding at Cana

Three days later there was a wedding at Cana in Galilee. The mother of Jesus was there, and Jesus and his disciples had also been invited. When they ran out of wine, since the wine provided for the wedding was all finished, the mother of Jesus said to him, "They have no wine". Jesus said "Woman, why turn to me? My hour has not come yet." His mother said to the servants, "Do whatever he tells you". There were six stone water jars standing there, meant for the ablutions that are customary among the Jews: each could hold twenty or thirty gallons. Jesus said to the servants, "Fill the jars with water". and they filled them to the brim. "Draw some out now' he told them "and take it to the steward." They did this; the steward tasted the water, and it had turned into wine. Having no idea where it came from - only the servants who had drawn the water knew - the steward called the bridegroom and said, "People generally serve the best wine first, and keep the cheaper sort till the guests have had plenty to drink; but you have kept the best wine till now". This was the first of the signs given by Jesus: it was given at Cana in Galilee. He let his glory be seen, and his disciples believed in him. After this he went down to Capernaum with his mother and the brothers, but they stayed there only a few days. (*Jn* 2:1-12)

The Third Mystery: The Proclamation of the Kingdom of God and the Call to Conversion

After John had been arrested, Jesus went into Galilee. There he proclaimed the Good News from God. "The time has come" he said "and the kingdom of God is close at hand. Repent, and believe the Good News." He was preaching the word to them when some people came bringing him a paralytic carried by four men, but as the crowd made it impossible to get the man to him, they stripped the roof over the place where Jesus was; and when they had made an opening, they lowered the stretcher on which the paralytic lay. Seeing their faith, Jesus said to the paralytic, "My child, your sins are forgiven". Now some scribes were sitting there, and they thought to themselves, "How can this man talk like that? He is blaspheming. Who can forgive sins but God?" Jesus, inwardly aware that this was what they were thinking, said to them, "Why do you have these thoughts in your hearts? Which of these is easier: to say to the paralytic, 'Your sins are forgiven' or to say, 'Get up, pick up your stretcher and walk'? But to prove to you that the Son of Man has authority on earth to forgive sins," - he said to the paralytic - "I order you: get up, pick up your stretcher, and go off home." And the man got up, picked up his stretcher at once and walked out in front of everyone, so that they were all astounded and praised God saying, "We have never seen anything like this". (*Mk* 1:14-15; 2:3-12)

The Five Mysteries of Light

The Fourth Mystery: The Transfiguration

He took with him Peter and John and James and went up the mountain to pray. As he prayed, the aspect of his face was changed and his clothing became brilliant as lightning. Suddenly there were two men there talking to him; they were Moses and Elijah appearing in glory, and they were speaking of his passing which he was to accomplish in Jerusalem. Peter and his companions were heavy with sleep, but they kept awake and saw his glory and the two men standing with him. As these were leaving him, Peter said to Jesus, "Master, it is wonderful for us to be here; so let us make three tents, one for you, one for Moses and one for Elijah." He did not know what he was saying. As he spoke, a cloud came and covered them with shadow; and when they went into the cloud the disciples were afraid. And a voice came from the cloud saying, "This is my Son, the Chosen One. Listen to him." And after the voice had spoken, Jesus was found alone. The disciples kept silence and, at that time, told no one what they had seen. (*Lk* 9:28-36)

The Fifth Mystery: The Institution of the Eucharist

It was before the festival of Passover, and Jesus knew that the hour had come for him to pass from this world to the Father. He had always loved those who were his in the world, but now he showed how perfect his love was. When evening came he was at table with the twelve disciples. Now as they were eating, Jesus took some bread, and when he had said the blessing he broke it and gave it to the disciples.

"Take it and eat;" he said "this is my body." Then he took a cup, and when he had returned thanks he gave it to them.

"Drink all of you from this," he said "for this is my blood, the blood of the covenant, which is to be poured out for many for the forgiveness of sins. From now on, I tell you, I shall not drink wine until the day I drink the new wine with you in the kingdom of my Father." (*Mt* 26:20, 26-29; *Jn* 13:1)

The Five
—Sorrowful Mysteries—

The First Mystery: The Agony in the Garden

They came to a small estate called Gethsemane, and Jesus said to his disciples, "Stay here while I pray." Then he took Peter and James and John with him. And a sudden fear came over him, and great distress. And he said to them, "My soul is sorrowful to the point of death. Wait here, and keep awake." And going on a little further he threw himself on the ground and prayed that, if it were possible, this hour might pass him by. "Abba (Father)!" he said "Everything is possible for you. Take this cup away from me. But let it be as you, not I, would have it." He came back and found them sleeping, and he said to Peter, "Simon, are you asleep? Had you not the strength to keep awake one hour? You should be awake, and praying not to be put to the test. The spirit is willing, but the flesh is weak." Again he went away and prayed, saying the same words. And once more he came back and found them sleeping, their eyes were so heavy; and they could find no answer for him. He came back a third time and said to them, "You can sleep on now and take your rest. It is all over. The hour has come. Now the Son of Man is to be betrayed into the hands of sinners.

Get up! Let us go! My betrayer is close at hand already." (*Mk* 14:32-42)

The Second Mystery: The Scourging at the Pillar

At festival time it was the governor's practice to release a prisoner for the people, anyone they chose. Now there was at that time a notorious prisoner whose name was Barabbas. So when the crowd gathered, Pilate said to them, "Which do you want me to release for you: Barabbas, or Jesus who is called Christ?" For Pilate knew it was out of jealousy that they had handed him over. Now as he was seated in the chair of judgement, his wife sent him a message, "Have nothing to do with that man; I have been upset all day by a dream I had about him". The chief priests and the elders, however, had persuaded the crowd to demand the release of Barabbas and the execution of Jesus. So when the governor spoke and asked them, "Which of the two do you want me to release for you?" they said, "Barabbas". "But in that case," Pilate said to them, "what am I to do with Jesus who is called Christ?" They all said, "Let him be crucified!" "Why?" he asked, "What harm has he done?" But they shouted all the louder, "Let him be crucified!" Then Pilate saw that he was making no impression, that in fact a riot was imminent. So he took some water, washed his hands in front of the crowd and said, "I am innocent of this man's blood. It is your concern." And the people, to a man, shouted back, "His blood be on us and on our children!" Then he released Barabbas for them. He ordered Jesus to be first scourged and then handed over to be crucified. (*Mt* 27:15-26)

The Third Mystery: The Crowning with Thorns

The governor's soldiers took Jesus with them into the Praetorium and collected the whole cohort round him. Then they stripped him and made him wear a scarlet cloak, and having twisted some thorns into a crown they put this on his head and placed a reed in his right hand. To make fun of him they knelt to him saying, "Hail, king of the Jews!" And they spat on him and took the reed and struck him on the head with it. And when they had finished making fun of him, they took off the cloak and dressed him in his own clothes and led him away to crucify him. (*Mt* 27:27-31)

The Fourth Mystery: The Carrying of the Cross

So in the end Pilate handed him over to them to be crucified. They then took charge of Jesus, and carrying his own cross he went out of the city to the place of the skull or, as it was called in Hebrew, Golgotha. Large numbers of people followed him, and of women too, who mourned and lamented for him. But Jesus turned to them and said, "Daughters of Jerusalem, do not weep for me; weep rather for yourselves and for your children. For the days will surely come when people will say, 'Happy are those who are barren, the wombs that have never borne, the breasts that have never suckled!' Then they will begin to say to the mountains, 'Fall on us!'; to the hills, 'Cover us'. For if men use the green wood like this, what will happen when it is dry?" Now with him they were also leading out two other criminals to be executed. (*Jn* 19:15-17; *Lk* 23:27-32)

The Fifth Mystery: The Crucifixion

When they reached the place called The Skull, they crucified him there and the two criminals also, one on the right, the other on the left. Jesus said, "Father, forgive them; they do not know what they are doing." Then they cast lots to share out his clothing. The people stayed there watching him. As for the leaders, they jeered at him. "He saved others," they said, "let him save himself if he is the Christ of God, the Chosen One." The soldiers mocked him too, and when they approached to offer vinegar they said, "If you are the king of the Jews, save yourself." Above him there was an inscription: "This is the King of the Jews". It was now about the sixth hour and, with the sun eclipsed, a darkness came over the whole land until the ninth hour. The veil of the Temple was torn right down the middle; and when Jesus had cried out in a loud voice, he said, "Father, into your hands I commit my spirit." With these words he breathed his last. (*Lk* 23:33-38, 44-46)

Near the cross of Jesus stood his mother and his mother's sister, Mary the wife of Clopas, and Mary of Magdala. Seeing his mother and the disciple he loved standing near her, Jesus said to his mother, 'Woman, this is your son'. Then to the disciple he said, 'This is your mother'. And from that moment the disciple made a place for her in his home. (*Jn* 19:25-27)

─ The Five Glorious Mysteries ─

The First Mystery: The Resurrection

After the Sabbath, and towards dawn on the first day of the week, Mary of Magdala and the other Mary went to visit the sepulchre. And all at once there was a violent earthquake, for the angel of the Lord, descending from heaven, came and rolled away the stone and sat on it. His face was like lightning, his robe white as snow. The guards were so shaken, so frightened of him, that they were like dead men. But the angel spoke; and he said to the women, "There is no need for you to be afraid. I know you are looking for Jesus, who was crucified. He is not here, for he has risen, as he said he would. Come and see the place where he lay, then go quickly and tell his disciples, 'He has risen from the dead and now he is going before you to Galilee; it is there you will see him'. Now I have told you." Filled with awe and great joy the women came quickly away from the tomb and ran to tell the disciples. (*Mt* 28:1-8)

The Second Mystery: The Ascension of Christ into Heaven

Now having met together, they asked him, "Lord, has the time come? Are you going to restore the kingdom to Israel?" He replied, "It is not for you to know times or dates that the Father has decided by his own authority, but you will receive power when the Holy Spirit comes on you, and then you will be my witnesses not only in Jerusalem but throughout Judaea and Samaria, and indeed to the ends of the earth." As he said this he was lifted up while they looked on, and a cloud took him from their sight. They were still staring into the sky when suddenly two men in white were standing near them and they said, "Why are you men from Galilee standing here looking into the sky? Jesus who has been taken up from you into heaven, this same Jesus will come back in the same way as you have seen him go there." (*Ac* 1:6-11)

The Third Mystery: The Descent of the Holy Spirit

When Pentecost day came round, they had all met in one room, when suddenly they heard what sounded like a powerful wind from heaven, the noise of which filled the entire house in which they were sitting; and something appeared to them that seemed like tongues of fire; these separated and came to rest on the head of each of them. They were all filled with the Holy Spirit, and began to speak foreign languages as the Spirit gave them the gift of speech. Now there were devout men living in Jerusalem from every nation under heaven, and at this sound they all assembled, each one bewildered to hear these men speaking his own language. They were amazed and astonished. "Surely" they said, "all these men speaking are Galileans? How does it happen that each of us hears them in his own native language? Parthians, Medes and Elamites; people from Mesopotamia, Judaea and Cappadocia, Pontus and Asia, Phrygia and Pamphylia, Egypt and the parts of Libya round Cyrene; as well as visitors from Rome - Jews and proselytes alike - Cretans and Arabs; we hear them preaching in our own language about the marvels of God." Everyone was amazed and unable to explain it; they asked one another what it all meant. (*Ac* 2:1-12)

The Fourth Mystery: The Assumption

We want you to be quite certain, brothers, about those who have died, to make sure that you do not grieve about them, like the other people who have no hope. We believe that Jesus died and rose again, and that it will be the same for those who have died in Jesus: God will bring them with him. We can tell you this from the Lord's own teaching, that any of us who are left alive until the Lord's coming will not have any advantage over those who have died. At the trumpet of God, the voice of the archangel will call out the command and the Lord himself will come down from heaven; those who have died in Christ will be the first to rise, and then those of us who are still alive will be taken up in the clouds, together with them; to meet the Lord in the air. So we shall stay with the Lord for ever. With such thoughts as these you should comfort one another. (*1 Th* 4:13-18)

The Fifth Mystery: The Coronation of Our Lady in Heaven and the Glory of the Saints

Now a great sign appeared in heaven: a woman, adorned with the sun, standing on the moon, and with the twelve stars on her head for a crown. (*Rv* 12:1)

I saw Mount Zion, and standing on it a Lamb who had with him a hundred and forty-four thousand people, all with his name and his Father's name written on their foreheads. I heard a sound coming out of the sky like the sound of the ocean or the roar of thunder; it seemed to be the sound of harpists playing their harps. There in front of the throne they were singing a new hymn in the presence of the four animals and the elders, a hymn that could only be learnt by the hundred and forty-four thousand who had been redeemed from the world. ...They follow the Lamb wherever he goes; they have been redeemed from amongst men to be the first-fruits for God and for the Lamb. They never allowed a lie to pass their lips and no fault can be found in them. (*Rv* 14:1-5)

And they cried out one to another in this way, "Holy, holy, holy is Yahweh Sabaoth. His glory fills the whole earth." (*Is* 6:1-3)

Further Reading

Marialis Cultus, Apostolic Exhortation, Paul VI, 1974.

The Secret of the Rosary, St Louis Marie Grignion de Montfort Treatise on The Devotion to the Blessed Virgin, St Louis Marie Grignion de Montfort.

Rosarium Viginis Mariae, Apostolic Letter on the Most Holy Rosary, John Paul II, October 2002.

Fatima in Lucia's own words, I, Postulation Centre, Fatima.

Endnotes

[1] Extracted from *Rosarium Viginis Mariae*, Apostolic Letter on the Most Holy Rosary, John Paul II, October 2002.

[2] Extracted from *Rosarium Viginis Mariae*, Apostolic Letter on the Most Holy Rosary, John Paul II, October 2002.

A set of Rosary beads.

A world of Catholic reading at your fingertips...

Catholic Faith, Life & Truth for all

CTS
www.CTSbooks.org

twitter: @CTSpublishers

facebook.com/CTSpublishers

Catholic Truth Society, Publishers to the Holy See.